12 REASONS TO LOVE
TRACK AND FIELD

by Todd Kortemeier

STORY LIBRARY

www.12StoryLibrary.com

12-Story Library is an imprint of Bookstaves and Press Room Editions

Produced for 12-Story Library by Red Line Editorial

Photographs©: Kyodo/AP Images, cover, 1; vivoo/Shutterstock Images, 4; Petros Giannakouris/AP Images, 5; mezzotint/Shutterstock Images, 6; Laszlo66/Shutterstock Images, 7; Library of Congress, 8; Matt Dunham/AP Images, 9, 10; Doug Mills/AP Images, 11, 29; Pete Niesen/Shutterstock Images, 12; Jae C. Hong/AP Images, 13, 28; Rainer Jensen/dpa/AP Images, 14; Marcio Jose Bastos Silva/ Shutterstock Images, 15; Pete Saloutos/Shutterstock Images, 16; Virginia Mayo/AP Images, 17; Lennox Mclendon/AP Images, 18; David J. Phillip/AP Images, 19; Christian Charisius/picture-alliance/ dpa/AP Images, 21; Diego Barbieri/Shutterstock Images, 22, 26; Joe Toth/Rex Features/AP Images, 23; sportpoint/Shutterstock Images, 24; jorome/Shutterstock Images, 25; Aspen Photo/Shutterstock Images, 27

Library of Congress Cataloging-in-Publication Data
Names: Kortemeier, Todd, 1986- author.
Title: 12 reasons to love track and field / by Todd Kortemeier.
Other titles: Twelve reasons to love track and field
Description: Mankato, Minnesota : 12 Story Library, 2018. | Series: Sports report | Includes bibliographical references and index. | Audience: Grade 4 to 6.
Identifiers: LCCN 2016047116 (print) | LCCN 2016054087 (ebook) | ISBN 9781632354310 (hardcover : alk. paper) | ISBN 9781632355003 (pbk. : alk. paper) | ISBN 9781621435525 (hosted e-book)
Subjects: LCSH: Track and field--Juvenile literature.
Classification: LCC GV1060.55 K67 2018 (print) | LCC GV1060.55 (ebook) | DDC 795.42--dc23
LC record available at https://lccn.loc.gov/2016047116

Printed in China
022017

Access free, up-to-date content on this topic plus a full digital version of this book. Scan the QR code on page 31 or use your school's login at 12StoryLibrary.com.

Table of Contents

Track Is an Original Olympic Sport 4

Reaction Time Is Fast 6

Jesse Owens Made World History 8

Some Events Test Many Skills 10

Sprinters Are the Fastest People on Earth 12

Marathons Are the Ultimate Test 14

Hurdles Make Races Harder 16

Some Runners Are as Good as Gold 18

The World Championships Are Exciting 20

Technology Gives Athletes an Edge 22

The Paralympics Let All Compete 24

High Jumpers Grab Big Air 26

Fact Sheet 28

Glossary 30

For More Information 31

Index 32

About the Author 32

Track Is an Original Olympic Sport

Track and field events are the most popular at the Olympics. They draw the biggest crowds during the games. Many exciting Olympians compete in track. They include Usain Bolt and Allyson Felix.

But before them, there was Koroibos of Elis. In 776 BCE, he won the first Olympic foot race in Greece. The race was 600 feet (183 m) long. Historians believe it was the only event in those Olympics.

The modern Olympics began in 1896. Only 12 track and field events for men were held that first year. Women's track was added in 1928. The current Olympic program started

Greece was home to the first modern Olympics in 1896.

People in Greece reenact the race from the original Olympics centuries ago.

in 2008. It features 47 track and field contests.

Some events have come and gone. The 60-meter sprint appeared in 1900 and 1904. It was dropped forever after that. In 1904 and 1920, there was a contest with a 56-pound (25-kilogram) shot put. Athletes today use much lighter 16.6-pound (7.3 kg) shot puts.

Other events have stood the test of time. As of 2016, all 12 events from the 1896 Olympics are still held. This includes the men's 100-meter dash and the men's marathon.

3
World records set at the 2016 Olympics in track and field.

- The first Olympic event was a foot race in Greece in 776 BCE.
- The modern Olympics began in 1896 and included track and field.
- Women's track and field was added to the Olympics in 1928.
- The current track and field program has 47 events.

US TRACK DOMINANCE

Since 1896, the United States has far and away been the best country in Olympic track and field. The United States has won 787 medals in the sport. Next closest is Great Britain with 203.

Reaction Time Is Fast

Every track and field race starts with a bang. It's the starting pistol. Once runners hear it, the race is on.

A lot has to happen after an athlete hears the pistol. The sound first reaches the runner's ear. The ear sends a signal to the brain. The brain then sends a signal to the legs to go.

Reaction time is the time it takes a runner to move after the pistol fires. The fastest sprinters' reaction

Runners take off with fast reflexes.

time is approximately 0.15 seconds. The average adult's reaction time is slower.

Reaction time is more important in sprints than in long races. Sprints are often decided by as little as a thousandth of a second. Every moment matters. Sometimes runners react even before the pistol fires. This is called a false start. A false start can knock a runner out of the race.

0.026
Seconds it takes the brain to signal the legs to move in an adult of average height.

- Every track race begins with a starting pistol.
- The best reaction time is approximately 0.15 seconds.
- A race can be won or lost due to reaction time.

THE STARTING "PISTOL"

In years past, a starting pistol was like an ordinary gun, only it didn't fire a bullet. It just produced a noise and white smoke. But at today's Olympics, the starting pistol is electronic. When the trigger is pulled, a light flashes. Then a signal is sent to the timing device. Finally, the sound of a gun is played. Each runner has a speaker on his or her starting block. That means they all hear the "shot" at the exact same time.

Starting pistols are now high-tech.

Jesse Owens Made World History

American track star Jesse Owens made history at the 1936 Olympics. The games were held in Berlin, Germany. Dictator Adolf Hitler ruled Germany at the time. Hitler believed Germans and other white people were the best athletes in the world. He didn't want black people to compete.

Owens grew up in the South. He was the grandson of slaves. By the time of the Berlin Olympics, he was already a star athlete. In 1935, he had broken three world track records in a 45-minute period. His long jump record stood for 25 years.

Owens became even more of a star at the Olympics. He won four gold medals. He won the 100-meter dash, the 200-meter dash, the 4x100 relay, and the long jump.

Jesse Owens's Olympic performance made history.

After his victory in the long jump, the first person to congratulate him was Luz Long, the silver medalist from Germany. Despite Hitler's beliefs, the German people cheered for Owens. When he returned to the United States, there was a parade in his honor in New York. In 1984, four years after Owens's death, a street in Berlin was named in his honor.

The people of Berlin named a street in Owens's honor.

10.3
Seconds it took Owens to run the 100-meter dash, which tied a world record.

- The 1936 Olympics were held in Berlin, Germany.
- German ruler Adolf Hitler believed only white people would win events.
- Track star Jesse Owens was black, and he won four gold medals at the games.
- Owens set multiple world records.

THINK ABOUT IT

Imagine being Jesse Owens at the 1936 Olympics. What would it feel like to win four medals when Adolf Hitler didn't want black people to compete? What pressure do you think Owens felt? What message did his wins send the world?

Some Events Test Many Skills

Competing in one track event is difficult. Imagine competing in an event that combines many events into one. For example, the decathlon features 10 events over 2 days. Its winner is often considered the greatest athlete in the world.

The running events in the men's decathlon are the 100-meter dash, the 400-meter dash, the 110-meter hurdles, and the 1,500-meter race. The throwing events are the shot put, discus, and javelin. Finally, decathletes compete in the long jump, high jump, and pole vault.

Ashton Eaton won gold in the 2016 Olympic decathlon.

the Olympics. Instead, women compete in the heptathlon.

The heptathlon has seven events. The pole vault and discus are dropped. The 400-meter dash and 1,500-meter race are changed to an 800-meter run. Scoring is similar. The 7,000-point barrier has only been cleared nine times. Six of those scores belong to American Jackie Joyner-Kersee.

Jackie Joyner-Kersee scored some of the best heptathlons in history.

Athletes score points based on how they do in each event. American Ashton Eaton set the world record at the 2015 world championships. He was one of two decathletes ever to top 9,000 points. He also won the gold at the 2012 and 2016 Olympics.

Men's and women's decathlons are nearly the same. Women run a 100-meter hurdle event. However, there is no women's decathlon in

8,893
Points Ashton Eaton scored in the decathlon at the 2016 Olympics, tying the Olympic record.

- Combined events, such as the decathlon and heptathlon, test different skills.
- The winner of the decathlon is considered the world's best athlete.
- Men compete in the decathlon at the Olympics, and women compete in the heptathlon.
- The decathlon has 10 different events, while the heptathlon has 7.

Sprinters Are the Fastest People on Earth

The 100-meter dash determines the fastest person on the planet. It lasts approximately 10 seconds, then it's all over.

The start is important. Runners begin with long, powerful steps. They stay low for 20 meters (66 ft). Then they run upright. Halfway through, they hit top speed. For the best sprinters, that's approximately 25 miles per hour (40 km/h).

Next, the sprinters slow. Still, they must keep up their technique for a strong finish.

In a flash, sprinters reach up to 25 miles per hour (40 km/h).

12

Seconds for Thomas Burke's winning 100-meter dash at the 1896 Olympics.

- The 100-meter dash showcases the fastest people on earth.
- The race lasts approximately 10 seconds for top sprinters.
- Sprinters' times have gotten faster over the years.
- Usain Bolt holds the men's record, and Florence Griffith Joyner holds the women's.

THINK ABOUT IT

Today's sprinters run the 100-meter dash much faster than Olympians a century ago. A century from now, do you predict times will have continued to fall? Or do you think there's a limit on human speed?

The men's record has been beaten often. The women's record has lasted longer. Florence Griffith Joyner's 1988 world record still stood through 2016. Her mark of 10.49 seconds has rarely been challenged. The closest time was Carmelita Jeter's 10.64 in 2009.

Runners lean slightly forward to cross the finish line. All these steps happen in a matter of seconds.

Both the men's and women's world record has dropped more than a second since 1912. At the 2009 world championships, Usain Bolt took it to a new low with a run of 9.58 seconds. He won gold at the 2008, 2012, and 2016 Olympics. Many experts believe he's the greatest sprinter of all time.

Usain Bolt is one of the greatest sprinters of all time.

13

Marathons Are the Ultimate Test

The marathon is a challenging race. It began when Philippedes, a Greek soldier, had to deliver a message. Greece had defeated the invading Persians. He ran 26 miles (42 km) from the town of Marathon to Athens.

The marathon has been an Olympic event since the 1896 games. The distance was set at 26.2 miles (42 km) in 1921. But marathons aren't just run at the Olympics. More than 1,000 marathons take place in the United States every year. A marathon is one of the toughest tests in track and field. For some, finishing the race is a challenge.

Dennis Kipruto Kimetto sets the world record for the marathon.

Tens of thousands compete in the Boston Marathon each year.

Dennis Kipruto Kimetto of Kenya holds the world record. He ran the 2014 Berlin Marathon in 2:02:57. That's less than five minutes per mile.

The Boston Marathon is one of the most famous marathons. Only 15 people competed in its first year of 1897. More than 30,000 people ran in 2016.

35,000
Gallons of water provided for runners at the Boston Marathon.

- A Greek soldier ran the 26 miles from Marathon to Athens.
- The marathon has been an Olympic sport since 1896.
- More than 1,000 marathons take place each year in the United States.
- The Boston Marathon is a famous race.

THE KENYAN CONNECTION

Men from the country of Kenya hold the record for 7 of the top 10 fastest marathons ever. Kenyan women have 4 out of the top 10. For some reason, Kenyans are amazingly good at distance running. There are several theories as to why. Many Kenyans train barefoot, which strengthens the feet. Kenya is at a high altitude. This means runners may develop the ability to take in more oxygen.

Hurdles Make Races Harder

Sprinting is hard enough. Add hurdles to jump over, and it becomes very difficult.

Hurdles can be anywhere from 30 inches (76 cm) to 42 inches (107 cm) high. Hurdle height depends on the level of competition. It also depends on the distance of the race. Because women tend to be shorter than men, women's hurdles are shorter.

Hurdle events are usually sprint races. But hurdles are also in the 3,000-meter steeplechase. In a steeplechase, racers jump several obstacles. Some hurdles have a shallow pool of water behind them.

A hurdler demonstrates proper form in the flight stage.

Steeplechase combines hurdles with water.

There are three steps to running hurdles. The first step is the takeoff. Runners keep up their speed as much as possible. They don't want to slow down when they get to the hurdle.

The next step is the flight stage. One leg comes up straight at the hurdle. The other leg passes horizontally over it. The goal in hurdles is to stay on the ground as much as possible. When runners jump, they don't move forward as fast. Another goal is to avoid touching or knocking over the hurdle. It isn't a penalty. But it slows the runner down.

The third step is the landing. Runners aim to land on their toes.

That allows them to keep driving forward. After that, it's time to prepare for the next hurdle. It could be only a second or two away.

10

Number of hurdles in a men's 110-meter event.

- Hurdles are obstacles to jump in a foot race.
- Hurdlers try to keep moving forward as fast as possible.
- Hurdling has three steps: takeoff, flight, and landing.
- Touching a hurdle is not a penalty, but it slows speed.

Some Runners Are as Good as Gold

In track and field, the biggest stage is the Olympics. It features the best of the best. Those who win gold are remembered forever.

Nobody has won more track and field medals than Paavo Nurmi. The Finnish distance runner won 12 total medals from 1920 to 1928. Of those, nine were gold.

Nurmi's nine gold medals are tied for the most of all time in track. American Carl Lewis also won nine golds. He has a silver as well. Lewis was a sprinter and long jumper. His first Olympics was in 1984. Even at age

Carl Lewis is one of three track Olympians tied for the most gold medals.

66
Countries that have won at least one gold medal in Olympic track and field history.

- Distance runner Paavo Nurmi has the most track medals in history.
- He is tied for the most gold medals with Carl Lewis.
- Allyson Felix has the most medals for women.
- Jackie Joyner-Kersee has the second-most women's medals.

THINK ABOUT IT

Athletes train four years between each Summer Olympics. Once their race begins, it may be over in a few seconds. How do you think athletes prepare their bodies and minds for years to do something that takes mere seconds?

Allyson Felix now holds the record for most gold medals for women in track.

35, Lewis won gold in the long jump in 1996.

At the 2016 Olympics, a third runner got close to the gold medal record in track. After winning three gold medals, Usain Bolt brought his career total to eight.

Also at the 2016 Olympics, American sprinter Allyson Felix won her seventh gold. That broke the record for most women's medals in track. Before Felix, American Jackie Joyner-Kersee had held the women's record since 1996. She won gold in the heptathlon in 1988 and 1992.

The World Championships Are Exciting

The Olympics get the big headlines. But track has another major competition. It's the International Association of Athletics Federations (IAAF) World Championships. The IAAF oversees track and field around the world.

The IAAF World Championships are not nearly as old as the Olympics. The first was held in 1983. Originally, it was held every four years. But it has been held every two years since 1991.

At the first world championships, 1,355 athletes from 153 countries participated. More than 2,000 athletes from more than 200 countries compete today.

Many world records have been set at the IAAF World Championships. With a time of 9.58, Usain Bolt set the world record in the 100-meter dash in 2009. He broke his own record of 9.69 seconds set at the 2008 Olympics.

The longest-standing record in track and field was set at the very first

19.19

Seconds it took Usain Bolt to run the 200-meter dash at the 2009 IAAF World Championships.

- The IAAF World Championships are a major international track and field competition.
- The first one was held in 1983.
- Many world records have been set there, including the longest-standing record in track.
- More than 200 countries watch the world championships.

IAAF World Championships in 1983. Czech Jarmila Kratochvílová ran the 800-meter event in 1:53.28. While some track records seem to be beaten at every competition, Kratochvílová's was still standing as of 2016.

As more countries compete in the IAAF World Championships, more people get a chance to watch them.

More than 200 countries were able to watch the event in 2015. In 108 countries, fans could even stream it online.

Track's best athletes give their all at the IAAF World Championships.

Technology Gives Athletes an Edge

Every fraction of a second counts in track. The latest technology and equipment can help athletes get an edge.

It starts where the foot meets the track. Spikes on today's shoes provide a huge amount of grip. The shoes themselves are also light.

New technology for the track helps, too. Athletes used to run on grass or dirt. Today's surfaces are made with a special type of rubber. It makes it hard to slip.

Technology has had a huge impact on the pole vault. Early poles were made of hardwood, bamboo, or aluminum. They didn't bend without breaking. Now poles are usually made of fiberglass or carbon fiber. These strong yet

Today's poles are made of materials that bend without breaking.

Sprinters use shoes with spikes that grip the track.

LIGHT ON THEIR FEET

Running shoes have come a long way in 100 years. Shoes in 1920 weighed approximately 10 ounces (283.5 g). They were made of leather. Today's shoes weigh less than three ounces (85 g). They are made of strong but flexible materials. Some runners don't use shoes at all. Christopher Koskei of Kenya won the 1995 world steeplechase with only tape on a few toes.

flexible materials let athletes spring themselves upward.

The Rio 2016 Olympics featured new technology. Some runners wore special tape on their bodies. The tape had little spikes on it. The spikes make the tape aerodynamic. That means the tape helps air move over the runner faster. Some runners also wore special sunglasses that let in only red light. This can calm athletes.

3

Maximum percent drop in wind resistance by using aerodynamic tape.

- Technology helps athletes get an edge over the competition.
- New shoes, track surfaces, and equipment help athletes.
- Runners used the newest technology at the 2016 Olympics.

23

The Paralympics Let All Compete

After World War II (1939–1945), many men returned home with injuries. Some had lost legs or arms. Some had vision problems. This led people to support adapted sports. In adapted sports, rules and equipment are adjusted so people with disabilities can play.

A small adapted sports competition was held alongside the 1948 Olympics. In 1960, the first Paralympic Games were held. Every four years, athletes with any number of physical disabilities can compete.

Track and field has been in the Paralympics since the beginning. The Paralympics feature nearly all the same track events as the Olympics. However, there is no decathlon or pentathlon.

Prosthetic blades help Paralympic athletes run nearly as fast as Olympic athletes.

- The Paralympics are the Olympics for people with physical disabilities.
- The Paralympics were first held in 1960.
- Most track and field events are the same as those in the Olympics.
- Events are adapted based on a person's ability.

Paralympic athletes are grouped by their disabilities. For example, athletes with visual impairment compete only against other athletes with visual impairment.

Each event is basically the same as in the Olympics. But the rules have been adapted so athletes with disabilities can play. For example, Paralympic runners who have lost limbs are allowed to use prosthetic ones. Some prosthetic legs are curved blades that spring off the track. Athletes without the use of their legs are also allowed to use wheelchairs.

Athletes with vision problems can use sounds to help guide them. In jumping sports, an athlete may have a coach call out when he or she should leap.

In adapted track, athletes with visual impairment run with the help of guides.

High Jumpers Grab Big Air

The high jump has been an Olympic event since 1896. Athletes run toward a bar set at a certain height. Then they launch themselves over it. The greatest high jumpers in the world today can jump higher than their own height.

The event has seen major changes over the years. In the past, jumpers used methods called the Eastern Cut-Off, Western Roll, and Straddle.

Then Dick Fosbury changed everything at the 1968 Olympics.

His method was to jump with his back to the bar. This allowed him to kick his legs up and over the bar. It looked as though he were bending backward over it. Fosbury won the gold medal that year. Soon high jumpers everywhere used the Fosbury Flop.

In 1993, Cuban Javier Sotomayor set the world record at 2.45 meters. As of 2016, that record has not been broken.

Many high jumpers use the Fosbury Flop method.

The women's record has lasted even longer. Stefka Kostadinova of Bulgaria jumped 2.09 meters in 1987.

Today's high jumpers can reach heights taller than most adults.

SOFTER LANDING, HIGHER JUMPS

For many years, high jumpers had to land in sand or sawdust. It was a hard landing. Jumpers had to use certain methods to protect themselves. Then foam mats were introduced in the 1960s. The softer landing made jumpers more confident to try new methods. The record went from 2.17 meters in 1960 to 2.29 meters by 1970.

6

High jump world records Valeriy Brumel set from 1961 to 1963.

- In the high jump, athletes try to jump over a bar.
- The "Fosbury Flop" changed the high jump in 1968.
- Both the men's and women's high jump records are among the longest-standing records in track.

27

Fact Sheet

- In the year 394 BCE, Emperor Theodosius I of Rome banned the Olympic games. After that, track and field nearly disappeared. It wasn't until the 1800s that the sport was revived in England.

- The IAAF was founded in 1912. But until 1936, it only oversaw men's track and field. Since the IAAF has included women's events, track has become one of the most popular sports for women.

- Foot races end at a finish line. Runners finish the race when their torso crosses the line. A head, hand, or foot doesn't count.

- In field events, such as the long jump or pole vault, athletes have more than one chance to perform. For example, a long jumper has three chances to clear a certain distance. Those who don't are eliminated.

- Track and field features the most events and athletes at the Olympics. In 2016, there were 47 events and 2,363 track athletes in Rio.

- Allyson Felix grew up with the nickname "Chicken Legs" because she was so lanky. She didn't join track until she was a high school freshman. But by age 18, she had won her first Olympic medal.

Glossary

adapted
Changed to fit a different purpose.

decathlete
An athlete who competes in the decathlon event.

dictator
A strict and controlling ruler of a country.

disability
An illness or injury that limits physical or mental abilities.

discus
A track and field event in which an athlete throws a flat disc.

impairment
A disability.

javelin
A track and field event in which an athlete throws a long spear.

prosthetic
A device made to replace a part of the body.

shot put
A track and field event in which an athlete throws a weighted ball.

sprint
A type of track and field race run over a distance of 400 meters or less.

Books

Amstutz, Lisa J. *The Science Behind Track and Field*. North Mankato, MN: Capstone, 2016.

Doeden, Matt. *Track and Field*. Mankato, MN: Amicus High Interest, 2016.

Labrecque, Ellen. *The Science of a Sprint*. Ann Arbor, MI: Cherry Lake, 2016.

Visit 12StoryLibrary.com

Scan the code or use your school's login at **12StoryLibrary.com** for recent updates about this topic and a full digital version of this book. Enjoy free access to:

- Digital ebook
- Breaking news updates
- Live content feeds
- Videos, interactive maps, and graphics
- Additional web resources

Note to educators: Visit 12StoryLibrary.com/register to sign up for free premium website access. Enjoy live content plus a full digital version of every 12-Story Library book you own for every student at your school.

Index

100-meter dash, 5, 8, 9, 10, 12–13, 20

Bolt, Usain, 4, 13, 19, 20
Boston Marathon, 15

decathlon, 10–11

Eaton, Ashton, 11

Felix, Allyson, 4, 19
Fosbury, Dick, 26

Greece, 4, 5, 14
Griffith Joyner, Florence, 13

heptathlon, 11
high jump, 10, 26–27
hurdles, 10, 11, 16–17

IAAF World Championships, 20–21

Joyner-Kersee, Jackie, 11, 19

Kenya, 15
Kimetto, Dennis Kipruto, 15
Kostadinova, Stefka, 27
Kratochvílová, Jarmila, 21

Lewis, Carl, 18–19

marathon, 5, 14–15

Nurmi, Paavo, 18, 19

Olympics, 4–5, 7, 8–9, 11, 13, 14, 15, 18–19, 20, 23, 24, 25, 26
Owens, Jesse, 8–9

Paralympics, 24–25

reaction time, 6–7

starting pistol, 6, 7
steeplechase, 16, 23

technology, 22–23

About the Author

Todd Kortemeier is a journalist and children's author from Minnesota. He has written more than 50 books for young people, primarily on sports topics. He and his wife live in Minneapolis.